KICKIN' IT with BESSIE

By: Makenzie Lee-Foster

Makenzie Lee-Foster

I'm a young author that wants to encourage other children to love reading and to follow their dreams. You're never too young to have big dreams!

My team....

...Forever and always.

I saw a cool coin inside of a store.
Everything about it was intriguing.

I took that coin everywhere! On the swing and even bike riding.

Then, I noticed something very strange. Lucky things started happening to me!

First, I found a $2 bill on the side of the road.

I used it to buy ice cream
for Josie and me.

I put a hat on Josie's head
and snuck her in with
the crowd.

I thought that nothing could go wrong because the coin was the luckiest thing around.

I guess that's the end
of our lucky streak, Josie.

It just disappeared withought
a trace to be found.

Could it be that things aren't as bad as they seem?

Remember when I found this amazing shirt? It was the last one and the perfect size for me!

How about that time we saved for months to buy the coolest toy we had ever seen?

We rushed home and opened up the box
to find a gold limited edition surprise pony!

When we found a huge pearl in a shell underneath the sea!

Or the time I had to kick a game
ending goal!

If we compare our luck before and after that coin, we might see something very interesting.

My luck had nothing to do with that coin. My luck is simply ME!

_____
(Print your name)

Do you have something that is very special to you?

_____

- -

- -

- -

- -

Where did you get it? What makes it so meaningful to you?

- -

- -

- -

- -

- -

What Makes You Special And Unique?

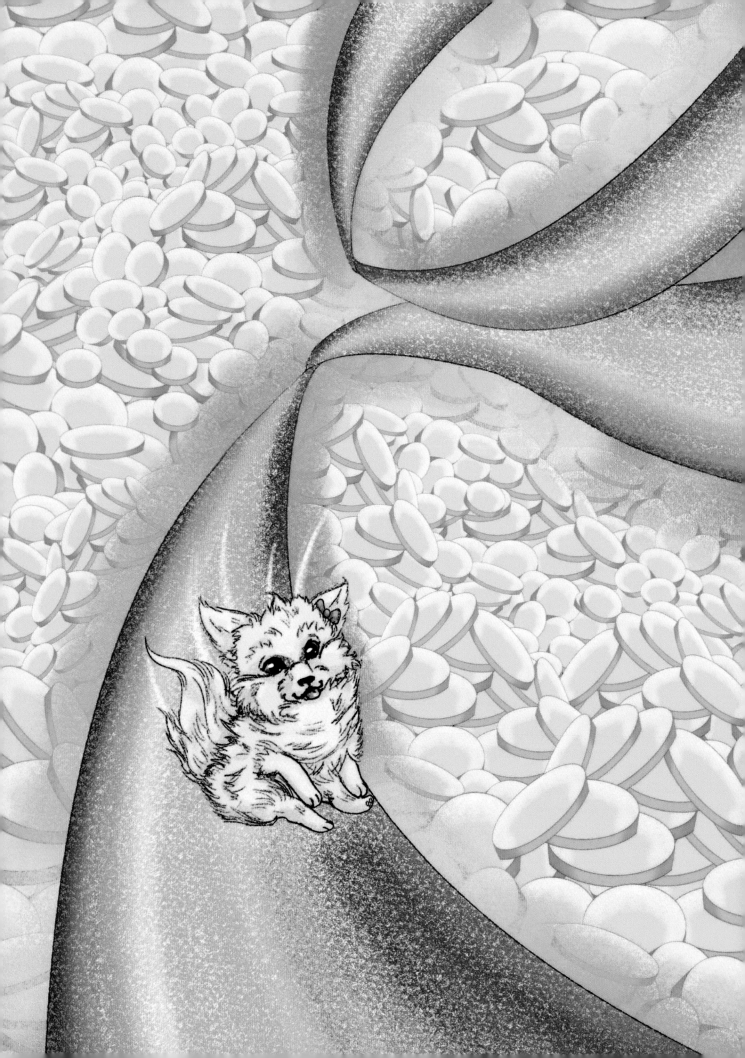